Hippos

Victoria Blakemore

Copyright info/picture credits

Cover, Uryadnikov Sergey/AdobeStock; Page 3, on-kelramirez1/Pixabay; Page 5, adege/Pixabay; Page 7, MarcoPomello/Pixabay; Page 9, eyespics/Pixabay; Pages 10-11, lisa_moertelbauer/Pixabay; Page 13, UTOPIA/AdobeStock; Page 15, fedetorres070/Pixabay; Page 17, evaschlomberg/Pixabay; Page 19, Tatiana Grozetskaya/AdobeStock; Page 21, camerawithlegs/AdobeStock; Page 23; mrmunky/AdobeStock; Page 25, monikawl999/Pixabay; Page 27, fotografie/Pixabay; Page 29, waldiwkl/Pixabay; Page 31, Uryadnikov Sergey/AdobeStock; Page 33, scooterenglasias/Pixabay

Table of Contents

What Are Hippos?

Hippopotamuses are large mammals. They are often just called hippos.

In ancient Greece, they called the hippo a "river horse" or "water horse." This is because they are almost always seen in the water.

Size

Hippos are the third largest land mammal. They can grow to be over sixteen feet long and five feet tall.

Adult female hippos often weigh about 3,000 pounds. Male hippos can weigh up to 9,900 pounds.

The pygmy hippopotamus is the smallest kind of hippo. It weighs less than 1,000 pounds.

Physical Characteristics

Hippos have very strong jaws and teeth. Males can use them to fight other male hippos over their **territory**.

Hippos have special nostrils that they can close. This is helpful when they are in the water so they don't get water in their nose.

Hippos have a special

membrane that can cover their

eyes. This allows them to see

when they are underwater.

Habitat

Hippos are found in rivers and lakes. They need water that is deep enough for them to be covered. They also need to be close to grasslands for **grazing**.

In the dry season, they are often found in muddy waters. They have to keep their skin wet or it could crack.

Hippos are found in parts of

central and southern Africa.

They are often seen in countries

like Kenya, Botswana, Rwanda,

Uganda, and Zambia.

Diet

Hippos are **herbivores**. This means that they only eat plants.

Their diet is mainly made up of grass and fruit. They can eat about 88 pounds in a single day.

Hippos usually come out in the late evening to graze when it is cooler. They spend about six hours each day grazing.

Predators

Hippos are so large that they

are safe from most **predators**

when they are adults.

Young hippos have to watch

out for predators like

crocodiles, lions, hyenas,

and leopards.

Young hippos also have to watch out for adult hippos who may fight. The adults can hurt them by mistake.

Communication

Hippos use sound to communicate with other hippos. They can tell where other hippos are and where their territories are by sound.

Hippos have a special fatty area in their neck. It allows their sounds to travel through air and water at the same time.

Hippos are often heard making a call that sounds like a honk. They also yawn a lot, which can be used to scare other animals off.

Movement

On land, hippos have been recorded running up to nineteen miles per hour.

Although they spend most of their time in the water, hippos can't swim. To move in the water, hippos bounce along the ground.

Hippos can hold their
breath for up to five minutes
under the water.

Staying Cool

Hippos have a special adaptation that keeps their skin from getting sunburned.

Their body makes a special red liquid that is called "blood sweat." It covers their skin and keeps them from getting burned.

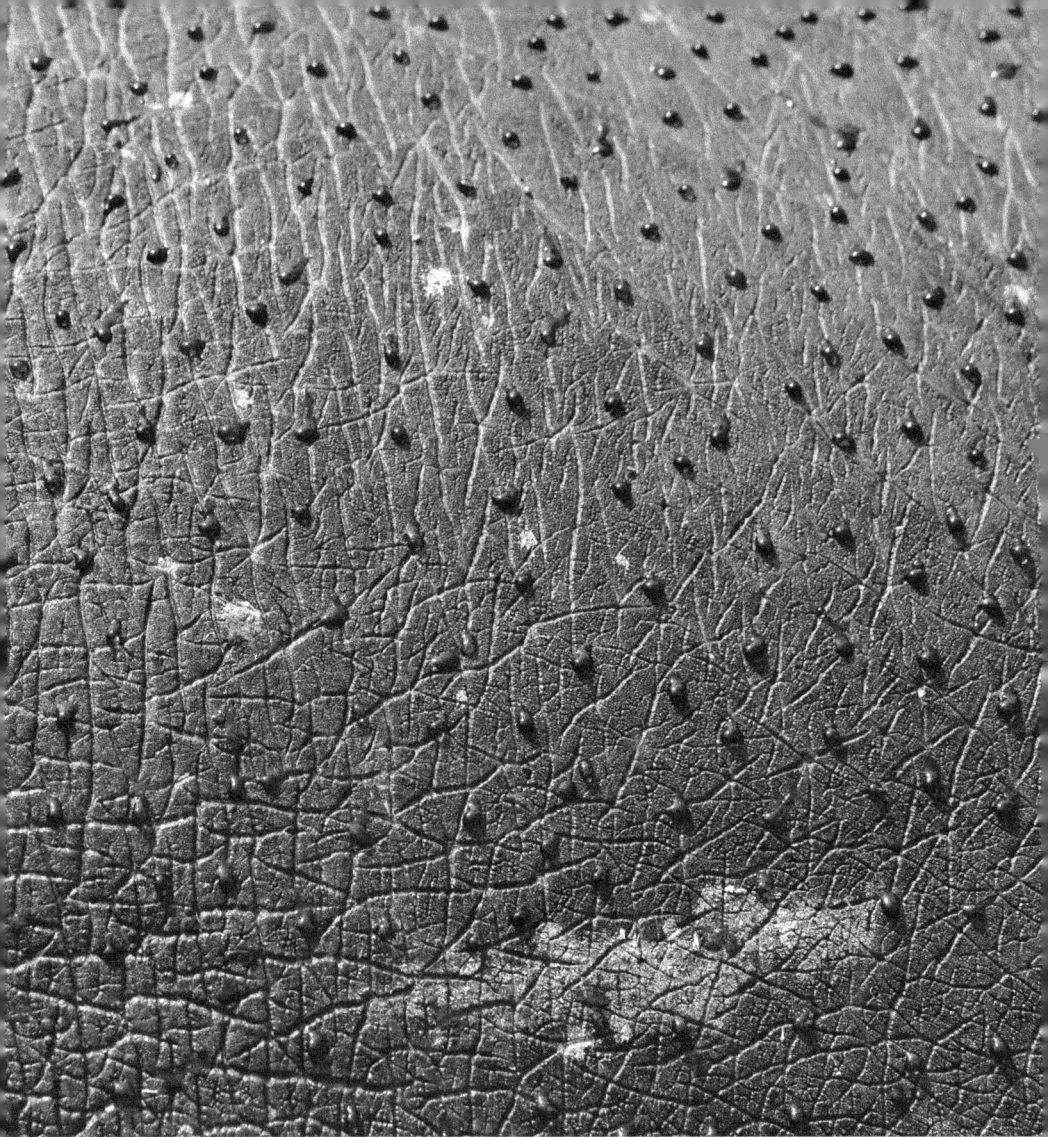

The liquid is called blood sweat

because it is red and looks like

sweat. It is not really blood or

sweat.

Social Life

Hippos are very social animals. They live in groups that are called herds, pods, or bloats.

The groups usually have between 20 and 30 hippos. There have been groups with as many as 200 hippos.

Hippos spend a lot of their time resting together in the water.

Hippo Calves

Hippos have one baby, or calf.

When they are born, calves usually weigh between fifty and 110 pounds.

Calves may be born on land or in the water. If a calf is born in the water, the mother must help it come to the surface to breathe.

A calf spends the first few

weeks of it's life with its mother.

Then, they rejoin the herd.

Self Defense

Hippos can be very **aggressive** animals. They are very **territorial** and do not like when people or other animals get too close.

If a person or animal does get too close, a hippo may charge at them. Hippos can bite, ram, and trample other creatures.

Hippos are one of the most
dangerous animals on earth.
They will attack people who
get too close.

Population

Common hippos are listed as **vulnerable**. Pygmy hippos are **endangered**.

Hippo habitats are being destroyed and **polluted**. Hippos are hunted by humans for their hides and tusks and because they threaten farmer's crops.

In the wild, hippos often live

between forty and fifty years.

Helping Hippos

Groups such as the African Wildlife Foundation are working to provide safe habitats for hippos.

Parks like the Lower Zambezi National Park are protected areas. Hippos there are safe from hunters and habitat destruction.

Groups are also working with communities close to hippo habitats. They are building fences and ditches to keep hippos away from crops and people.

The hope is that safe habitats and keeping hippos from people will help their populations to increase.

Glossary

Aggressive: mean, unfriendly, ready to fight

Endangered: at risk of becoming extinct

Grazing: feeding on grass

Herbivore: an animal that eats only plants

Membrane: a thin layer of tissue, a thin covering

Polluted: when a habitat is full of waste or trash

Predator: an animal that hunts other animals

Territorial: when an animal will fight over it's territory

Territory: an area of land that an animal claims as its own

Vulnerable: an animal that is likely to become endangered

About the Author

Victoria Blakemore is a first grade

teacher in Southwest Florida with a

passion for reading.

You can visit her at

www.elementaryexplorers.com

Also in This Series

Gray Wolves	Sloths	Flamingos	Camels	Koalas	Honey Bees	Pandas
Pangolins	White-Tailed Deer	Orcas	Giraffes	Corn	Meerkats	Echidnas
Walruses	Raccoons	Bald Eagles	Apples	Arctic Foxes	Red Pandas	Cassowaries
Tigers	Ladybugs	Moose	Beluga Whales	Leopards	Elephants	Jellyfish
Binturongs	Lions	Dolphins	Reindeer	Hammerhead Sharks	Hippos	Pumpkins
Peafowl	Chameleons	Florida Panthers	Aye-Ayes	Black Bears	Cheetahs	Manatees
Gingerbread	Polar Bears	Hot Chocolate	Orangutans	Coyotes	Marshmallows	Strawberries

Victoria Blakemore

Also in This Series

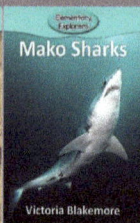

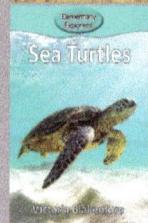

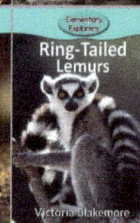

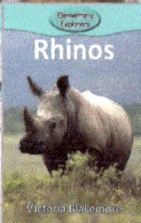

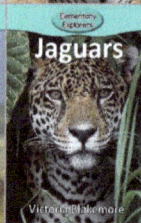

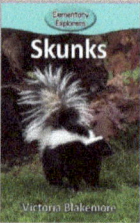

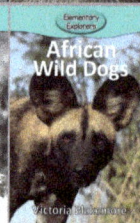

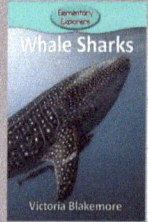

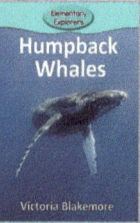

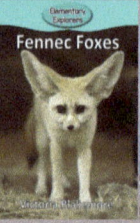

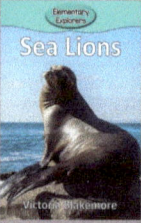

Aardvarks	Mako Sharks	Alligators	Frogs	Hedgehogs	Brown Bears	Bongos
Sea Turtles	Quokkas	Muskrats	Zebras	Red Foxes	Ring-Tailed Lemurs	Platypuses
Anteaters	Kangaroos	Rhinos	Jaguars	Wombats	Capybaras	Gorillas
Cats	Skunks	Butterflies	Dingoes	Snow Leopards	African Wild Dogs	Penguins
Whale Sharks	Wolverines	Warthogs	Caracals	Badgers	Seals	Hummingbirds
Pikas	Humpback Whales	Pumas	Lemonade	Llamas	Tulips	Ostriches
Sunflowers	Fennec Foxes	Sea Lions	Squirrels	Roses	Porcupines	Ice Cream

All cards labeled: Elementary Explorers · Victoria Blakemore

www.ingramcontent.com/pod-product-compliance
Lightning Source LLC
Chambersburg PA
CBHW051252020426
42333CB00025B/3166